# The HAMPER & TRIVET CATALOG

PHIL

JAKE

*"Offering a Complete Line of Unique, Innovative, Electronic, Digital American Products."*

## IT'S INCREDAFFORDABLE!

BY MARK DROP AND STEVEN SPIEGEL

•

ILLUSTRATIONS BY MICHAEL LABASH
*Contest Winner from the Previous Edition of Our Current Catalog*

•

DESIGN BY JACKIE SEOW

•

A FIRESIDE BOOK
PUBLISHED BY SIMON & SCHUSTER, INC.
NEW YORK

A Fireside Book

Published by Simon & Schuster, Inc.

Simon & Schuster Building

Rockefeller Center

1230 Avenue of the Americas

New York, New York 10020

FIRESIDE and colophon are registered trademarks of Simon & Schuster, Inc.

Designed by Jackie Seow

Manufactured in the United States of America

10  9  8  7  6  5  4  3  2  1

Library of Congress Cataloging-in-Publication Data

Drop, Mark.

  The Hamper & Trivet catalog.

  "A Fireside book."

  1. Mail-order business—Anecdotes, facetiae, satire, etc.  2. Catalogs,
Commercial—Anecdotes, facetiae, satire, etc.  I. Spiegel, Steven.  II. Title.
III. Title: Hamper and Trivet catalog.

PN6231.M17D76  1986      818'.5407      86-12116

ISBN 0-671-61132-1

# The HAMPER & TRIVET CATALOG

PHIL

JAKE

*"Offering a Complete Line of Unique, Innovative, Electronic, Digital American Products."*

# A Personal Message from Phil Hamper & Jake Trivet

Dear User:

We all love leafing through "wish books" like these, but what a thrill it is to actually *buy* something from one. Shopping at home is more than a thrill, it's your *right* as an American, a duty, a privilege that people in many less-fortunate countries just don't share. Unfortunately, not all Americans can exercise their right to shop at home; after all, how many of us can really afford that $3,000 for a cat-shaped blender? As Abe Lincoln probably once said, "Not me."

Well, we here at Hamper & Trivet feel that *every* American should be able to shop at home, browse casually, and pick an item (or items) at his or her leisure. Imagine *never* having to leave your fine home, to look for a parking place, to call ahead and see if "they" have what you're looking for, to cart the kids around—never having to endure *any* of those tiresome shopping chores. Never *ever*. Wow! Life sounds better already, doesn't it? When a person shops at home he's in touch with his full potential as an American. Perhaps as a human being. And we want to help everyone reach that point.

So we offer a full line of unique, innovative, electronic, digital American products. And here they are! An entire catalog chock-full of exciting-looking gifts for *you*, the would-be shop-at-home public: appliances for the modern kitchen, technology that brings the house alive with beeping noises, furnishings that fill your fine home with places to sit. In short, something for every room in the house, from the garage to your head. And not a single one available in any store! Others may try to copy our gifts, but every item herein was invented, developed, tested, and used by *us* (except the stuff for women), something other so-called catalogs cannot boast.

And get this! You don't have to be rich to shop with us. You can enjoy the thrill of buying a brand new gift item at a fraction of the cost shown, through our unique Hamper & Trivet Payment System. That's right; we charge only what you can afford, leaving you feeling like money is just so much green paper to be tossed about. And most of all, we leave you with enough left over to shop with us again.

It's that incredible. That affordable. We call it INCREDAFFORDABLE!

Welcome to the exciting American pastime of shopping at home! We hope you enjoy sending in orders as much as we enjoy receiving them. As you browse, remember that had our forefathers known about catalog shopping they most certainly would have included *it* as one of our in-alienable rights!

Appreciatively yours,

*Phil Hamper*

*Jake Trivet*

**Phil Hamper & Jake Trivet**

# The Hamper & Trivet Story

Fifteen years ago I (Phil) was standing in an unemployment line when I heard a man behind me groaning and wincing, seemingly in pain. "Something wrong?" I asked. "Oh, no. I'm fine. And I've got my keys," he replied. My quizzical look pressed him to explain further. "You see," he said, "although I pay rent, I spend a lot of my time on the street, simply because I'm always losing my keys. So I invented this . . ." He pulled from his pocket a large, sharp-edged, cumbersome hunk of iron with several keys dangling from it. "It helps me remember I've got them. If I leave without them, I notice my leg isn't puffy and sore and I turn around and pick them up."

"It's sort of a reminder that you don't have your keys?" I ventured. "Sort of a 'key-minder'?"

After thinking that one over, Jake—that was his name—agreed that that was what it was. "You're a genius," I said. "You ought to market that thing. You'd make a million!"

Kicking at the floor bashfully, he admitted having little marketing sense. Then, perceiving a grand opportunity, I quickly added that I DID have a background in marketing, having just been let go from the local Foodworld. We laughed at what a coincidence that was, and went our separate ways.

Five years later, I was waiting for an elevator on the way to a job interview. The elevator arrived, opened, and appeared to be completely full. "I'll wait," I mumbled under my breath. The doors began to close, then suddenly sprang back open. "Hamper? Is that you?" I heard from behind the crowd. "Jake? Jake Trivet?" I replied. Sure enough. There he was, folding up the fiberboard replica of a crowd of people and slipping it neatly into his briefcase.

At that point I knew for sure this guy had a mind for ingenious inventions. I didn't let him get away this time. I walked him to the nearest coffee shop where, over eggs and juice, we etched out our plans for a mail-order company, strictly catalog, that would make these incredible inventions of his available to the public.

Now, here we are, several years and hundreds of items later, running a booming direct-mail business. And although we've become a prosperous company, us two guys still receive, process, and ship all orders ourselves.

Of course, Jake doesn't invent every item we offer. But he oversees the research and development of new items while I handle the marketing aspect of the business.

We appreciate your patronage and the fact that you shop with us. We believe these gifts are one of a kind and that's what makes them unique. We challenge you to find a similar collection of gift and household items. Go on, we dare ya. If you do, don't tell us. It would just depress us.

Now, sit back in your easy chair, pour yourself a cup of tea, let it steep, put your feet up, let your shoulders relax, and ahh . . . BUT DON'T CLOSE YOUR EYES! We wouldn't want you to miss a single item from our HAMPER & TRIVET collection of fine "Giftables" . . .

# Hello Cruel World!

Get down off that ledge and hand us the gun. You don't have to off yourself because of life's crummy problems. Fight back with these life-made-easier products.

## EMBARA-SHIELDS STALL BLINDS

Public stalls suffer one fatal design flaw—they don't reach the floor, leaving a person's identifiable feet visible to all beneath the stall (and don't kid yourself, everyone knows what shoes you're wearing!)—making the possibility of sex perverts, precocious kids, or clumsy people scrambling for dropped change crawling under your door horrifyingly real. Well, Stall Blinds make that constant fear of embarrassment a thing of the past. Portable fold-up curtains attach magnetically to any metal stall door and wall, cordoning you off in complete privacy. Ahhh! Available in Black, Grey, and Marble-ette. Graffiti available, please specify. HT1900—$160.95.

## MICRO-ROT OVEN

Americans hate eating any food that's not "perfect." That half to-mato, that leftover tuna salad: these are things we'd rather not bother with. Especially if a NEW tomato or an unopened can of tuna is sitting on the shelf ready to be used. Don't throw away perfectly good leftovers and burden yourself with visions of starving children. Spoil it first. Throw those leftovers into the Micro-Rot Oven, and—*phfft!*—they're spoiled, leaving you with rotten gar-bage that "no one—even people in Third World countries—could eat." Then, go ahead and use that *new* tomato or unopened can of tuna for a guilt-free meal! This little device is a *must* for all Ameri-can households. HT10000—$769.95.

## KEY-MINDER

Modern man has one major security blanket—his key chain. We've all experienced that sudden panic, followed by that pat-patting gesture. What a bother! Now let your key chain remind you itself! This 13-lb. hunk of wrought iron, studded with sharp spikes and inlaid with pointed steel edges, won't ever let you forget your keys are right where you put them. Sharp pains and puffy, discolored bruises are a constant reminder that all's secure. Comfort signals . . . you've lost your keys! HT1700—$110.95.

## SOCK TRACKING SYSTEM

There's nothing more frustrating than losing one sock in a pair. And it happens so often! Well, no more. This space-age tracking system, originally developed by NATO to track enemy aircraft and missiles, keeps you briefed on the location of every sock at all times. Small, magnetically charged "chips" sewn into each sock signal the Present Sock Location (PSL) to a master sensing device back on the base (your fine home). PSL is pinpointed with blips on the "big board." (your TV!). HT9800—$890.95 complete.

## THE BANK CADDY

If you hate wasting precious time filling out forms at the bank counter when you could be standing in line moving toward the tellers, then this is for you! Simply hook this patented timesaver over the shoulders of the person in line in front of you and fold down the desk flap to place day/date calendar, pen-on-a-chain, and all necessary bank slips within easy reach—while holding your place in line! Available in three styles: smoked glass (ultra-modern branch), white plastic (high-tech automated branch), Italian marble (stodgy conservative branch). HT8700–$339.95.

## CAREER SCREEN PROJECTOR

You're thinking about changing careers, but, well, you don't know if it's the right move. There's a simple way to find out. How would you look as a member of that other field? Look into our patented "mirror-system" and see how you'd look dressed in the regalia of a judge, a nurse, a soldier, the President—200 careers in all! Comes complete with 200 mirrors, each painted with the uniform of a different career. Why take chances with your future? Simply stand in front of the Career Screen and find out if you're "cut out" for another line of work. HT68000—$45,987.95.

PHIL and JAKE

## ONE OF OUR FAVORITES

*We like all our items. We like this one a little bit more.*

### "SORRY ALL FULL" ELEVATOR CROWD

There's nothing like riding the elevator all the way to or from your floor *alone*. But it was a rare treat until now. Use the H & T "Sorry All Full" Elevator Crowd and you're an easy rider. This hinged "Crowd" unfolds to fit in the doorway of most elevators. When the door opens, simply call out over the "passengers," "Sorry all full!" Works every time! Folds to fit most briefcases. HT1100—$759.95.

# *Women and Children...Second*

No, your fine home isn't sinking! We just thought it would be considerate to put these items for women and children up in front.

## HAT TRAY

Face it. Your children *are* going to sneak downstairs and invade your cocktail party, no matter how hard you try to stop them. So why not put 'em to use, with a set of these deluxe Hat Trays? Strap-on trays hold up to 12 drinks, or two plates of pizza rolls, tiny three-corner sandwiches, whatever! Guests will grin and comment on how cute and helpful the little rug rats are, and you'll have more time to "mingle." Get one for each child. HT900—set of 2¼ trays—$198.95.

*Another fine gift for your head.*

## ADULT SUPERVISION

Now you can be spared the hassle of keeping an eye on your kids while they play with hazardous things. We'll send you a full-grown, legal adult to keep an eye on the kids all day long. Give your "ball and chain" that BB gun or those firecrackers they whine for and just sit back and relax. Adult Supervision also comes in handy for those insipid PG and R movies the kids want to see but you don't. Comes complete, no assembly required. HT98800—$98,007.95 plus room and board.

## WOODEN PANTSUIT

Limited edition! Pure Dutch walnut. Fine craftsmanship and super finish. No two alike! Be the envy of somebody, somewhere. HT2900—$789.95.

## CUT-OUT TV KID WARDROBE

Turn on any prime time sit-com. See all those spiffy-looking kids? Look at them. Prancing around in great sweaters and pleated pants *you* can't even afford! Now look over at your kids. And you thought you were keeping up with the Joneses! Your kids need a wardrobe, and they need one bad! Well here's a quick answer until you save the millions needed for a *real* TV wardrobe. Just cut out the outfit desired, fold the tabs over junior's shoulders, and—presto!—your kid's got a dashing fashion sense! It's that simple. Specify "young star" or "hot starlet." HT1100—$569.95 complete wardrobe.

## SKIN-LIKE-NEW

A beauty milestone, this latex-based complexion spray keeps those unsightly blemishes, acne pimples, scars, and freckles out of sight. Simply spray it on before you leave the house and, hey, your skin looks great! Smooth, shiny, manageable. Caution: do not use near eyes, nose, or mouth. And *never*, under any circumstances, cover entire body! HT400—$45.95 per can.

## CHORE-BOTS

Lure your kids into thinking you're being nice by giving the gift of Chore-bots. Exciting-looking robots just like on Saturday morning TV...only these robots don't turn into trucks, or planes, or giants; they convert into a washer and dryer set, dish-sink and disposal, a lawn mower...a whole family of household help machines! They didn't have toys like this when you were a kid. Thank God! HT4400—$679.95 each.

# Gifts Make Better Presents!

## NEWSWEEK COVER STORY

For a nominal fee, the entire staff of *Newsweek* reporters waits at the ready to work up an entire cover feature (including photos) about YOU or someone on your gift list. Any topic will do: your favorite night spots, an apartment you fixed up, dishes you like to prepare. Now, through this H & T exclusive offer, you can have an entire newsmagazine devoted to you! They don't do stories on everybody! So be sure to pad your chances with this offer today. HT6700—$4,000.95.

## FRENCH FRY SAMPLER

There are millions of different fast-food chains, each with its own deliciously different French fry recipe. Not to mention the handsome designs on those fry cartons. Mmmm. Hamper & Trivet Gift Sets introduces the French Fry Sampler, a large decorative box holding 25 different food-chain brands of golden brown fries, each in its own authentic fry carton. This is your chance to sample the tasty gamut of that fast-food staple, the French fry—each one crispy on the outside, tender and delicious on the inside. Just pop 'em in the microwave! Order today and we'll rush your sampler via fourth class mail —book rate. Great holiday gift idea. You'll be remembered long after the last fry is gone. HT1500—$86.95.

## TELESCOPING BRIEFCASE

Hey, we know how hard it is to set down your briefcase in a crowded train, bus, or elevator. All that stooping and bumping into other people! Eww! So we set our minds to developing this back saver. Push a button and the space-age handle "telescopes" (up to 200 feet), setting the case on the floor with virtually no effort on your part. "Voilà!" Your hand is free to scratch, dig for keys, anything! This high-tech tote comes in black leather, brown leather, or teak. HT5700—$600.00.

# Bells are Buzzing

Ding dong, the witch is dead! The witch we called Ma Bell. Now everyone can make and sell phone equipment. And if everyone's doing it, that means we are too! Take a look . . .

## SANS-A-RING PHONE

Tired of your phone's annoying loud ring? The Sans-A-Ring Phone signals at such a low frequency it can't be heard by the naked ear. No one hears it but you, thanks to a surgically implanted vibro-plate which sends electro-impulses shooting through your cerebral cortex. A migraine headache tells you you've got a call! Penetrates walls, reaches for blocks in all directions. You must arrange to be flown to the Hamper & Trivet "clinic" for micro head-surgery. A simple operation—really. HT8800—$5,600.95.

## GERM-AWAY PHONE DEFENDER

So many people use your phone every day. Even people you don't know! Just think of all those germs and diseases they're breathing onto your phone's receiver! Well, wipe it off and start anew with the Germ-Away Phone Defender. An armlike device snaps onto the actual receiver, keeping possible germ carriers at bay. They'll have to shout to be heard, but at least you'll be safe from infection. Get one today, before you get something you didn't pay for! HT1600—$387.95.

*Another fine gift for your head.*

## PHONE STRAP

Hands-free phoning . . . don't dream of it, own it! Handy strap system fits most American phones that aren't shaped like imaginary animals. The Phone Strap loops easily around your head so you can cook, sew, watch TV, smoke, or take medication without the bother of holding a receiver aloft for an infinite amount of time. Straps are made of a comfortable cotton/wool blend. It's like wearing no phone at all! HT1200—$201.95.

## ELECTRO-NET ANSWERING MACHINE

Networking is an important part of life; don't be left out! Here's a machine that leads your friends to believe you're *the* person to know. Ingenious microchip technology is preprogrammed to leave messages in digitally synthesized human-sounding voices. Just play back your daily "messages" when friends are within earshot and let them overhear things like: "Hey, (name), thanks for the lead; I got the job at Shearson-American Express!" and "Say, thanks for letting me win at squash the other day. Are you still looking for a V.P. spot?" Please specify cute nickname. HT6800—$609.95.

# Give the Gift of Gifts!

## THE HEAD FOIL

Everyone worries about their hair, especially about getting it messed up before an important business meeting or date. That's exactly why H & T created The Head Foil. Simply place The Head Foil over your head and hair, wearing it as you would any ordinary hat. The Head Foil automatically deflects wind and dust particles up and over your head, leaving your hair just how you wanted it—neat! Pressed from lightweight Styrofoam. HT4500—$129.95.

## GRAM-O-GRAM

A guy named Paco will personally hand-deliver any message you want and an ounce of pure cocaine to friends, loved ones, and business associates. The perfect gift for that hard-to-shop-for addict on your list. HT9900—$7,000 in unmarked bills.

## THE YACHT TABLE

How many of you miss mealtime on the high seas? Well, fret no more! This ingenious invention simulates the rocking motion of a sailing vessel's galley. Spring-loaded legs give the illusion of eating at sea. This handsome table, carved from Norwegian driftwood, adjusts for calm waters, rough sailing, and typhoon. Comes complete with all the plates and silverware you need, anchored down to prevent messy spills. HT6000—$599.95.

# Book 'Em!

Not just ink and paper . . . these are books!

## THE CAVE FORMATIONS

This brand-new series is now available for the first time anywhere from Hamper & Trivet Press. Every cave formation is discussed in its own lavishly illustrated volume. Collect them both! Volume One: The Stalactites. Volume Two: The Stalagmites. Many pages each. HT300—one each month—$39.95. Receive entire set at once—$129.95.

## THE FULL POTENTIAL OF OUR NATION'S HIGHWAYS

It sure was smart of our government to design and build America's great superhighway system back in the 1950s, but these seemingly endless bands of concrete have been lying in wait for their full potential to be tapped. This book shows us virtually thousands of ways this system can be utilized more efficiently. Here are just a few: playing four square or shuffleboard, sharpening knives, or even drying fruit. Now we can finally start making the most of these engineering marvels! 800 pages plus ill. HT500—$111.95.

## SOVIET LEADERS AND THEIR ILLNESSES

This is the perfect gift for history buffs and political science students alike! This hard-bound reference book includes a large easy-to-read wall chart listing all Soviet leaders since the Revolution and the illnesses that claimed their lives. This fascinating volume will be turned to again and again as a family source book. It's invaluable! 389 pages. HT400—$160.95.

# ONE OF OUR FAVORITES

PHIL and JAKE

*We're proud to have developed these two new reference books, helping students get a head start in the world of words.*

H & T has just published these two ground-breaking reference volumes: *What Words Mean* and *Words That Mean the Same Thing as Other Words.* Leatherbound. 1350 pages each. HT1200—$250.95 each; $575.95 for both.

## SUGAR PACKET CHEAT BOOK

Boy, do you look stupid! You took the boss out to dinner and he stumped you with a trivia question about the first airship! You could have prevented the whole mess—by referring to your handy Sugar Packet Trivia Cheat Book. Contains over 12,000 commonly known facts frequently presented as trivia on sugar packets in thousands of our nation's restaurants. They're all here. Women in history. Aviation. Historic Schooners. Fits secretly in the palm. Never again feel the fool at dinner. HT200—$103.95 a copy.

## HAMPER & TRIVET'S HOME FIX-IT SERIES

This lavish collection has taken years of compiling and now can be yours. Each volume contains priceless information on getting more out of your home. For example, turn that old damp basement into . . . a hospital. Make your spare room into a drycleaner's! The kids have moved out? Well turn their old room into a deli. And look at that living room; you never use it. Now make it work for you. Turn it into a profitable funeral parlor! These books show you step by step how to turn your house into a thriving network of profit centers. We'll start you off with the first volume—*From Den to Shoestore*— for just $49.95. Then you'll receive another lavishly illustrated volume each month, containing handy hints on obtaining licenses and "obeying" zoning laws. Don't miss out on the financial potential of your fine home. Order today! HT1200—$395.95. Entire library of 12 books.

## BOOKS ON TAPE

Wrap gifts, repair torn pages, seal envelopes . . . all while reading the greatest books ever written! You'll never miss a word; they go by one at a time. All those classics you never read, but felt you should have. Now you can catch up on *Moby Dick*, *A Tale of Two Cities*, *Hollywood Wives*, all while doing odd little chores around the house. What a way to read! Hey, you're not taking time out from a thing, and you're reading the classics, too. Complete library (30 books) on 30 rolls. HT1400—$784.95.

## WRITING AND SELLING YOUR MENUS

You're a struggling writer with a million ideas buzzing around your head. All you need is a way to organize your thoughts, put them down on paper, and sell them to whoever will buy. We'll let you in on a secret. You won't get anywhere writing short stories, articles, plays, or poems. Millions of frustrated typists are already hacking away at that stuff. Let us show you a real way to turn your writing into big bucks . . . with menus! This step-by-step approach to writing creative, easy-to-read menus in numerous genres—from Greek Coffeeshop to Natty Seafood Joint—includes chapters like "Personifying the Foodstuffs," "How Cute Should You Be?" "Do Bad Line Drawings Help?" "101 Names for the Meat Sandwich," and more. Also included is a helpful "Menu Agent Index"—listing the men and women whose job it is to sell menus to restaurants in need. It's their job to know when a restaurant is looking to upgrade its menu, or about to open a new location. Why wait? You can be on your way to a new career in six to eight weeks! HT800—$98.95.

# *Sphere Delights*

Round and round we go! Where do we stop? High-quality spherical gifts.

*Another fine gift for your head*

## "GREENHOUSE" COMPLEXION GLOBE

Does the winter wind and cold dry out your skin? Sport this lightweight Complexion Globe featuring what scientists call "the greenhouse effect." The sun's warming rays penetrate the globe, and, unable to bounce out, steam up the globe with weather—moisturizing your skin as long as the sun is out. Large enough to accommodate your favorite winter hat. Order one today, and let the magic of the greenhouse rain on your face. HT500—$1,523.95.

## GLOBES OF THE FIFTY STATES

The United States. Formed over 200 years ago with the blood, sweat, and tears of our forefathers. The United States. A nation that has spawned such ideals as "All men are created equal," and "Life, liberty, and the pursuit of happiness." The United States . . . now you can own them! Not one, not two, not even three, but all 50 states sitting proudly in your den, home, or rec room. Imagine owning a living testament to your belief in the American Way. Imagine

no more. Now, exclusively from the Hamper & Trivet Mint come the Globes of the Fifty States. Each state painstakingly handcrafted onto a beautiful globe 6 inches in diameter. It's as if each great state of the union had its own planet! Adorn your shelf with 50 different globes. 50! Count 'em! Each mounted on a polished brass stand that will handsomely display your patriotism for all to see. And each globe is hand-enameled in three all-American colors: cherry-tree red, Valley Forge white, and skies-of-freedom blue. Each is engraved with the issue date and your favorite name. Each comes with its own certificate of authenticity. And each certificate of authenticity comes with *its* own certificate of authenticity so you can be sure everything is authentic. Each globe depicts the geographic boundaries, points of interest, and number of Stuckey's in each state.

But that's not all! If you order today, you'll receive, at no additional cost, globes of Puerto Rico and Grenada. No, they're not states yet, but they're still *ours!*

Every other month, you'll receive another handsome collector's item. You'll cherish these fine globes as learning tools, decorative bookends, conversation pieces. Or fill them with candies, hang them from the ceiling, and beat them with a stick. Whatever you do with them, we know you'll enjoy these globes for generations to come.

Let Hamper & Trivet Mint enhance your world today. HT9800— Entire set of 52 globes: $1,679.95.

## PENGUIN GLOBE

Educational, accurate, adorable. Now our Earth comes shaped as everyone's favorite member of the animal kingdom. You've got the salt shakers, you've got the bookends, now have the world! HT3500—$367.95.

Dear Guys.

I love your catalog. I especially like your spherical items. I'm in the hospital and the spherical items are the only ones they let me get on account of I stabbed my wife and children eight years ago. Please keep offering them or I don't know what I'll do.

Lars Nifgrid
Bellvue Hospital
New York, NY

# "Gift" Almost Spells "Give"

## SHOPPING PROD

There are few things more embarrassing than asking some strikingly realistic mannequin where the men's department is. So we created this ingenious little face-saver—a two-foot "wand" that holds 12 "D" batteries and dispenses a mild electric shock. Simply touch the arm of any suspected dummy before asking for help. If it's a real person, well, you certainly have their attention. If not, you've hurt nothing—especially your pride! Order one for each member of the household. HT4700—$298.95 each; batteries not included.

## USA TODAY HOLDER

You know you actually read *USA Today*. You find the one-column stories on foreign policy informative, the full-color photos engrossing, the Stats-At-A-Glance enriching, and the four-color weather map invaluable. Yeah, you know that. And we know that. But do *they* know that? Don't just sit there and take those funny looks, angry stares, or even hurled objects. Order the USA Today Holder —a mock-up copy of a real newspaper that slips easily over the front of "America's Newspaper." Then, relax and enjoy the paper you *want* to read. It *is* a free country. Please specify *Wall Street Journal, New York Times, Washington Post.* HT1300—$67.95.

## ONE OF OUR FAVORITES

### DRINKING GLASS DRINKING GLASSES

These classy glasses will be remembered and talked about long after your party is history! Each drinking glass is embossed with a different type of drinking glass. They're all here: the Mug, the Stein, the Highball, the Juice, and the Martini. Five drinking glasses in all! Bottoms up! HT3000—Set of 5 glasses: $123.95.

*We're both drinking-glass enthusiasts from way back, so you can bet we each own display collections of this exquisite glassware in our fine homes.*

# We've Got You Covered!

So don't try anything funny. You've got the right to use a charge card on these fine items that cover you and your possessions. Anything you buy can and *will* be billed to you.

## AD STICK 'EMS

Everyone loves magazines. But we all hate to wade through page after page of obnoxious advertisements. We suggest Ad Stick 'Ems, pretty patterned adhesive panels that blot out annoying ads in your favorite periodicals. Just peel 'em off and stick 'em on. Avoid being subtly brainwashed by the ruthless ad perpetrators we've got running loose in America. 50 Ad Stick 'Em sheets (enough for close to two magazines!). HT1100—$98.95.

## TERRY CLOTH SUIT

Ah, the roar of the surf, the call of gulls, and the smell of salt air; it's business as usual for executives on either coast. Don't be left out. Be prepared for your next beach meeting with this soft and supple terry-cloth three-piece suit. Comfortable, absorbant, and great looking. Order several. Available in Green, Red, and Chess/Backgammon Pattern. HT9800—$399.95.

## ART GUARDS

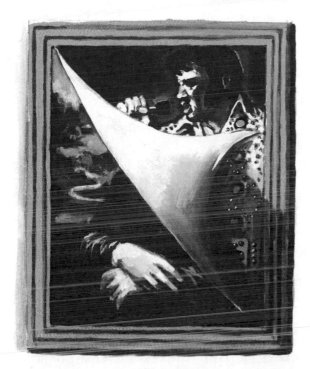

Doctors' and dentists' offices all across the country have found a way to protect priceless paintings without the cost and hassle of insurance or security. It's also an easy and inexpensive way to protect art treasures at home. Art Guards are self-adhesive shades that roll down over your fine art, revealing the world's most undesirable paintings. Available in Elvis, Tiger, and the Tall Ships. All in black velvet. No self-respecting crook would touch 'em. Please specify sizes. HT6800—$812.95.

## "OLDE TYME RADIO" SIMULATOR

It's eight o'clock, the table is cleared, and the family gathers around . . . the radio? In the '80s? Absolutely—thanks to our clever "olde tyme" radio facade. Simply snap the false chassis onto the front of any television set and enjoy your favorite TV programs *without a picture!* What a thrill. Just like in the "olden" days. Bring your family closer together. Improve imagination skills. Order one for each set in the house. HT500—$679.95.

## WHOLE WHEAT COMFORTER

Whole wheat. We all know its nutritional value, but did you know it also can keep you snuggly warm? We've stuffed this soft cottony comforter with all-natural whole wheat. No additives. No preservatives. Nothing but whole wheat goodness. Also available in cracked grain and 100% bran. HT6600—$300.95.

## TILE RAINCOAT

The people that build bathrooms aren't dumb. They use tile on the walls for a reason—it's waterproof. What better material could there be for use in the ultimate rain slicker?! Hundreds of small, decorative tiles cover you with a fairly flexible surface that just plain *won't absorb water!* You'll never be drenched again. And this coat will last and last. Cleaning: Just hose it down. Do not use abrasive cleansers. HT7800—$492.95.

## KNIT GUN MITTENS

You're asleep. Suddenly you are awakened by an intruder prowling around downstairs. You reach to the night table for your gun and . . . it's icy cold! That problem's gone forever with Hamper & Trivet's own Knit Gun Mittens. Keep your trigger

toasty warm with these cozy hand-knitted comforters. Available in three embroidered messages: "Home Safe Home," "A Man's Gun Is His Castle," and "All's Well That Ends in a Hail of Lead." HT1200—$56.95 each.

## H & T'S BIG SHIRT

Fashion goes haywire! The race to have the biggest shirt has been won . . . by *us!* Hamper & Trivet introduces the BIGGEST shirt. Starched canvas, French cut, pleated back, button-down collar, extra-strong button stitching, available in a variety of stripes and colors and 15 yards across! Protect your lawn from frost, keep leaves out of the pool—the adventuresome might try wearing it! HT3600—$465.95.

# All Tied Up

The tie. The quintessential gift. The gift of gifts. The king of gifts. Here, made that much more special. Give the gift they can't return. We promise we won't take them back.

## BREAK-AWAY SAFETY TIE

Your heart is racing, pulse pounding . . . the silk tie you're wearing is caught between two elevator doors! Their vice-like grip won't let go! What do you do? Too bad you're not wearing a "safe tie"— namely the Hamper & Trivet Break-Away Safety Tie. Give a firm tug just above the perforated line and—zip!—Velcro technology sets you free. You'll never worry again about garage doors, biting dogs, meat grinders, or trash compacters. Neckties are dangerous: don't take chances. Order several today. Available in stripes, paisley, and the Tall Ships. HT300—$79.95.

## MICROTHIN TIES

Thin ties have *never* been thinner! Measuring a slim 1.2 mm, these ties could be in the Guinness Book of World Records. Give any wardrobe a "mod" look. Come in three hard-to-discern patterns: stripes, paisley, and the Tall Ships. Cool! HT500—$29.95 each.

## BERMUDA TIES

When you're on vacation the last thing you want to do is dress up for dinner or a night on the town. Now turn your most casual vacation wardrobe into dazzling evening-wear with these classy Bermuda Ties. In the tradition of Bermuda shorts, these very short ties come in *outrageous bright plaid* patterns, in only the very slickest of synthetic materials. Order several. HT900—$67.95 each.

# Hamper & Trivet . . . It's Short for Gifts!

J.P. MORGAN

*Phil —*
*A couple new ideas:*
*— Cardigan stacks?*
*— Toilet brittle?*
*What do you think*
*— Jake*

## REFRIGERATOR MAGNATES

With a twist! What red-blooded American blue blood wouldn't love small plastic brass-looking busts of famous American magnates on their fridge door—holding up bank statements, IOU's, maybe even personal notes or photos? There's Onassis, the shipping magnate; Carnegie, the steel magnate; Henry Luce, the publishing magnate; and old "King Oil" himself, Rockefeller. Forget fruit and Ziggy! Here are some refrigerator magnates with *class!* Eight in all. Collect 'em. HT800—$79.95 each.

## SECURITY SCULPTURE

In a special arrangement with noted pop sculptor George Segal, Hamper & Trivet offers incredibly lifelike sculptures of YOU. Place them in strategic places in and around your home and then take off on that cruise or golf vacation you've been planning without worrying about your fine home or valuables. Your sculpted likenesses keep thieves and vandals in their own bad neighborhoods! Amazing! When you're at home, the sculptures make great coat trees. Please advise us **THREE YEARS** prior to scheduled vacation. HT10000—Each family member: Priceless.

# It's on the House!

No, these products aren't free. They go ON your fine home.

## HOME MARQUEE

Americans in pursuit of an easily identifiable house number will go to any length! Painting their curbs. Hanging huge plastic or brass numbers beside their door. Naming their homes with cute wooden signs. Why not call out your address much more effectively and with a lot more class? Install the Home Marquee and let everyone know that you and your family are "now showing." Easily suspends over your front door so no one, not even a nearsighted mailman, can help but know who lives there. Plus, the 3,000 watts of illumination help make the neighborhood safe. HT37000—$3,659.95.

## ROLLTOP SIDING

In the battle to keep ahead of the Joneses, nothing scores as big as getting new siding. So imagine the advantage you'd have if you could change your siding at will . . . That's where Rolltop Siding comes in. Installs over existing brickwork (or stuccowork), then, as a rolltop desk reveals a workspace and pigeonholes, this fine siding slides up or down to reveal an utterly different facade! Amazing! Helps confound persistent bill collectors. HT10800—$4,590.95 installed.

## NATIONAL MONUMENT KIT

Hundreds of flea-bitten get-rich-quick schemes are offered through the mail, but ours is the classiest! The Hamper & Trivet Historical Society will send you everything you need to turn *your* home into a national monument. Imagine all the revenue from concession stands, souvenir shops, tours. And the tax breaks are phenomenal! You get 50 yards of red velvet rope and eight shiny poles, assorted brass-like plaques, attention-getting bunting, and a secret dossier that shows you how to make your home qualify. Special sections include: Huge Roadside Animals and How to Build Them, So Where Do They All Park?, and Cotton Candy vs. Popcorn: The Controversy Rages. HT1500 — Entire kit: $1,354.95.

# About Our Store

You can't actually visit our store. The only store we have is in your hands. Just imagine this book as having four walls, brightly colored linoleum, fluorescent lighting, and busy clerks merrily stocking our intriguing gifts on corrugated metal shelving. Imagine...

Look over there! There's old Herb, the security guard, relaxing by the automatic doors. "Hi, Herb! How's it going? That's nice. See you later." Boy! That was a close one. He almost pulled out the pictures of his kids.

Now let's roam the wide, spacious aisles and find what it is we're looking for. What's that? Oh, you've spotted a Hamper & Trivet Special. Let's take two, they're such a deal! Yes, you're right: it *is* easy to find everything you're looking for in this comfortable shopping environment.

Let's take our purchases to the friendly cashier. Her name is Cheryl. She goes to the local high school and is at Hamper & Trivet on a work-study program. You may know her; she might babysit for you on the weekends. That's because Cheryl's not just a person who's good at what she does, she's a *good* person. And that's the kind of person we would hire...if we had a store.

So we pay for our items and head jauntily out the automatic doors to our waiting car. "Bye, Herb! Have a nice day!"

There. Now you've been to our store. Thanks for coming and we'll see you again real soon.

# Gift Certificates

We offer our own unique version of gift certificates. Well, sort of. Here's how it works. You specify the denomination you'd like to give the "giftee"—either $5, $10, or $20. We then send that person, along with a copy of our latest catalog, a crisp bill in that very denomination, all in a handsome Hamper & Trivet Giftvelope. They'll never forget you remembered.

# Special "Glow-In-The-Dark" Option

You're probably saying, "Wow, what a great catalog, how could they ever improve on it?" Ask no more. For a mere $30 extra, EVERY ITEM in this catalog can be ordered with a glow-in-the-dark option. Simply hold your order under any ordinary light bulb for 60 seconds, turn off the lights and WOW! IT GLOWS! Please specify on our handy order blank.

# Extra Special Penguin Option

A Hamper & Trivet exclusive! After extensive research, we have found that the penguin is America's most popular gift shape. So, for an extra $25, any item in our catalog can be pressed, cut, or stamped into the shape of a penguin! We can't guarantee that all the items will work this way as effectively . . . but won't they be cute?

# The Hamper & Trivet Guarantee

Every one of our items comes with the special Hamper & Trivet LIFETIME GUARANTEE of satisfaction. We guarantee that if you're not 1,001% satisfied at any time with *any* Hamper & Trivet product, simply let us know, and we'll send you an authorized, hand-written letter of apology.

# Ordering Instructions and Contest Rules

Ordering from us couldn't be simpler! Or easier! Just write your name, address, city, state, and zip code in the order blank below. Figure up your total cost (see SPECIAL NOTE ON PRICING below). Then simply draw the items as you envision them on a separate piece of paper, and return it with the order blank. YOU DO NOT HAVE TO BE AN ARTIST TO ORDER FROM HAMPER & TRIVET. A simple thumbnail sketch will do. However, the customer who best renders our fine products will win the opportunity to illustrate next season's Hamper & Trivet Catalog! That's right. You could have the prestige of your name gracing the Hamper & Trivet Catalog cover. You could experience the thrill of your art being seen by men, women, and people all across America!

And, best of all, you're entered just by ordering from us! Isn't that easy? No complicated forms to fill out. No gold stickers to peel and place. No celebrity heads to punch out. Jake and I are the sole judges and we're super impartial. Any relatives of ours are not eligible because we've already used them. So good luck and Godspeed! We're right behind you.

The Mood Desk

## Special Note on Pricing

In order to make the joy of shopping at home that much more joyful, ALL THE PRICES LISTED FOR OUR FINE PRODUCTS ARE FAKE. Do you really think we'd charge you, our loyal shop-at-home customer, such outrageous fees for our lovely products? NO WAY! This is just our patented way of making you feel like one of the elite—those people with so much money they don't know what to do with it. Don't worry, we know you're not stuck up. To order, all you need to know is that the Hamper & Trivet order number that precedes every price, is the price. Got it? Simply change the HT to a $ (dollar sign) and place a decimal point in front of the last two 0's. It's that easy. It's that simple. It's that inexpensive.

$. 3000

---------- **ORDER BLANK** ----------

# The Hamper & Trivet Lecture Series

We are available to speak on a wide variety of subjects on which we are experts. Perfect for marketing seminars, workshops, high school classes, craft bazaars, and church services. Our lectures are entertaining, inspirational, and loads of fun.

Jake's special workshop, THE BATHROOM: AN INVENTOR'S THINK TANK, is perfect for kids ages zero to one hundred and zero! It's an entertaining seminar that lets imaginative youngsters and oldsters in on Jake's "best kept secret."

Phil's seminar, STAYING IN SHAPE IN THE '80s, is great for anyone who's overweight or just trying to tone down.

Best of all, this is a free service. We love to speak, and you'll love having been spoken to!

(NOTE: Please specify if you want us to glow in the dark during our seminars.)

If you don't have the facilities to host a Phil and/or Jake workshop/seminar we are also available on video cassettes. It's virtually the same as having us in person only the special effects are better. Please specify VHS or BETA.

Other available programs: Hidden Marketing Secrets of the Tall Ships; Penguins ARE Profitable; and The Head: An Untapped Profit Center.

# Nice Guys' Furniture Lasts

Hamper & Trivet. A couple of nice guys, right? And guess what? Our furniture lasts! Make your living room worth living in with these lovely pieces . . .

## PORT-O-PIT

"A conversation pit makes the home." What is a home without a sunken area filled with pillows where people can exchange witty banter, delve into deep philosophical questions, or "get in touch" with their feelings. Ahh, that's living. But what happens when you're out camping, or on a cruise, and want to strike up a rap session? That's when this portable conversation pit can come in handy. Pull the inflation tab and—FOOM!—you're sitting around talking and sipping brandy . . . whatever! Made of sturdy vinyl. Body-hugging contour. Fits 7 comfortably. HT5300—$3,525.95.

## BIZ-Z-BOY ARM CHAIR

Every wife who has a lazy hubby around the house will *love* the Biz-Z-Boy Arm Chair. Give it as a gift and rest assured he won't be lounging around when there's house or yard work to be done. Incredibly uncomfortable design makes it nearly impossible for the man of the house to settle in and enjoy the game . . . let alone that book he's been wanting to read. Things'll start getting done once and for all thanks to this grueling piece of furniture. Ingenious . . . yet subtle! HT3000—$980.95.

## TEAK REFRIGERATOR STAND

You've got an appliance stand for your TV/VCR units, and a stand for your stereo components. About the only appliance in your home not protected by wood and smoked glass is your refrigerator. Or is it? Your icebox can be just as well off as your other electric devices simply by ordering this beautiful teak case. The touch-sensitive smoked glass doors retard fingerprints. The hardwood chassis prevents scratches and dents. The easy-roll casters make for effortless movement. Don't leave your fridge out in the cold. HT2700—$856.95.

## SCIENTIFICALLY DESIGNED THROW PILLOWS

A miracle of modern science threatens to make ordinary throw pillows obsolete. You've always thought that the throw pillow was one of nature's perfect designs. How could anybody improve on it? Well, leave it to Hamper & Trivet to do just that! The basic flaw in all throw pillows is that they never land on your couch perfectly every time you throw them. Well, we've revolutionized the throw pillow, bringing it into the '80s by computer-designing the ultimate pillow that WILL LAND PERFECTLY EVERY TIME. No more fluffing. No more adjusting. These pillows will land perfectly when thrown from any distance. The perfect gift for that "comfort-loving" person on your list. Available in velvet, corduroy, and denim. HT4200—$209.95.

## ORIGAMI FURNITURE

Now you can take the ancient art of folding paper and sit on it! You receive large sheets of cardboard perforated in exact detail. Chippendale, Queen Anne, and Ethan Allen styles available. Furnish an entire dining room with a 2' x 8' sheet! Easy instructions make you a master of this ancient art in minutes. Never polish again. HT1200 —$3,097.95.

## TRACK AND FIELD LIGHTING

Lighting fixtures race along electric tracks circling your living or rec room. Set up hurdles. Team different fixtures against one another! Makes for challenging competition! Easily installed with screwdriver, pliers and computerized hydroelectric lathe system. HT11100—$879.95.

## MOOD DESK

This antique-like desk changes woodtones to reflect the temperament of the person sitting behind it. An excellent gift for the boss! You'll know if the time is right to ask for that big raise. Easy to read. Changes from Oak to Maple to Pine to Formica. Enhances almost any decor, occasionally. HT20800—$1,879.95.

## THE ULTIMATE COFFEE TABLE BOOK

This book with legs is a must for every living room. A conversation piece, an objet d'art, and a real big book all rolled into one piece of functional furniture! Assembly required. Choice of two books: *North American Men with Beards* and *Celebrity Clefts*. HT2700— $879.95.

PHIL and JAKE

# ONE OF OUR FAVORITES

*Now that we're direct-mail bigshots, we couldn't afford not to own several.*

## "YOUR OWN" NEW YORK APARTMENT

Don't feel like a loser because you live west of the Hudson—get that New York Apartment you've always wanted. These authentic domiciles are mined from actual N.Y.C. walk-ups. Fits easily in any regular-size apartment. Authentic touches add realism—cracked walls and warped floors; shower, sink, stove, and toilet all in the same room. Be the envy of all your comfortable friends. Three views available: Uptown, Downtown, the Tall Ships. HT12700— $3,500/mo. plus deposit and $1,000 H & T finder fee.

# The Men's Room

Hey, shut that door! Can't you see this is the men's room? All you'll find on these pages is fine clothing for the man of the house.

## TUPPERWARE® SHIRTS

You love the way Tupperware® locks the freshness in around the kitchen, and you hate having your shirt come untucked halfway through a busy day. That means you'll love this latest fashion advancement! The shirt snaps into the matching groove on your Tupperware® belt and you're in business. It doesn't come untucked until you want it to. Then, just pull the tab and—swish!—it's open. No more messy spills—and it's dishwasher safe! HT2800—Shirt and belt: $167.95.

## TRIVIAL BLUE SUIT

Everyone's favorite game comes to the office! This finely tailored 100% wool garment has hundreds of mind-boggling trivia questions sewn right into the lining. Everyone's playing it, now you can wear it! HT8900—$895.95.

## TURKISH PRISONER UNIFORM WITH CAP

The Turkish authorities don't take prison lightly, and neither do the makers of Turkish incarceration garments, like these we smuggled out on the backs of thieves, rapists, and even close friends. To be sure, the rough texture of the burlap is more uncomfortable than any piece of clothing you've worn before. We figure it doubled as a comforter for napping in solitary confinement. Wear it without shoes, though a sensible pair of loafers might make a nice match. Authentic whip marks adorn the back, and you'll find plenty of secret hiding pockets! This tough outfit from a tough country is for tough shoppers like you.

All of our "exporters" were sorry to part with their caps once reaching freedom (something to do with the cap being an excellent place to stow cash and other contraband). We had to use force to get these durable toppers from a few of the fellows. They weren't too sore; either they gave us the caps or we promised to make a trip back with a few "escapees" we "managed to round up." In the end, we got the caps and are passing them on to our free-and-happy-about-it-shop-at-home shoppers. HT4400—$457.95.

# It's My Hobby and I'll Buy If I Want To

Hobbies keep us out of jail, so they're good, right? Right! Here are some craft and hobby items to keep you and yours out of the slammer.

## THE SUBSCRIPTION CARD COLLECTOR STARTER KIT

We're all familiar with those annoying little postcards that magazines use to entice you to subscribe. "Blown" inside to lure your attention, all they really do is fall out and litter your home. Until now.

Subscription card collecting is the hobby of the future! Few realize the value of a 1976 *Time* magazine Christmas card (the one where the little magazines form a tree). Subscription card collecting is fun, decorative, and can be PROFITABLE. Now you can be in on the thrill and excitement with this sampler pack of cards from the '70s. 150 in all! But that's not everything! We'll toss in a decorative Sleekra® binder that's perfect for displaying these unique collectibles. But hold on a minute, we're not through yet!

You'll also get our unique guide book, *Subscription Card Collecting and You*, the definitive guide to the fascinating world of blow cards. Hundreds of full-color illustrations in this indispensable volume show you the rare and the medium rare. Warning: Once you get started collecting these handsome pieces of cardboard, you won't want to stop. Ever. IITI IUN– Kit: $808.95.

## HUMMEL DICTATORS

These pudgy miniatures are loving recreations of the most notorious world leaders of all time. Notice the fine detail on Stalin's mustache. Napoleon's rakish hat. The little upraised arm of Adolf you-know-who. They're all here. From Mussolini to Ghengis Khan. You'll find these detailed statuettes are perfect accents to any decor. Use the Shah of Iran and the Ayatollah Khomeini as the most ironic pair of bookends your friends, family, or loved ones will ever see! These li'l fellas are all very realistic—only shorter and cuter. You'll want to get them all. They're as collectible as "little Dutch kids"! HT1100 —$1,995.95 each.

## RECORD STORAGE SYSTEM

Hypersensitive about record care? Us, too. That's why we decided to develop this exclusive record storage system that keeps your priceless vinyl discs free from dust, finger prints, damage, and theft —not so much a product as a service we offer. Once enrolled in the service your entire collection will be kept in our private Long Island City storage facility. In this dust-free environment your records will be utterly safe . . . FOREVER. They'll never be handled by human hands again! Relax! HT300—$550.95 per crate per year.

   ***Also of note to music lovers! Ask about our huge selection of **USED RECORDS** at giant discounts. Hundreds and hundreds of artists available. Write for free price list.

## PHOTO ANTIQUER

There's nothing better than sitting on the porch enjoying a nice cold glass of lemonade and poring over antique photos. "That's great," you say, "but what if we don't have any antique photos?" Now your boredom is over! Simply take any family photo and presto! It becomes rich in history. First, paste on any of the hundreds of our "you were there" overlays, then brush on the brown antiquing liquid. Wait a couple of hours and . . . your family's history! Kit comes with everything you need to make great tin prints. You supply the photos. HT1400—$152.95.

Junior K.O's Schmeling in first round

Mom and Dad and the Hindenburg

# Are You Now, or Have You Ever Been, a Member of the Party?

We don't really care what your political leanings are. Why, we just want you to have a heck of a good time.

## CRUSHED ICE TRAYS

Nothing says "I've made it" better than serving crushed ice at a get-together. Used to be you needed large, noisy, expensive machines to make crushed ice at home. But not any more. These durable, lightweight PolySleekra® trays are a mere quarter of an inch thick, and are loaded with thousands of tiny chip-like divots. Crushed ice freezes in minutes. It's a party! HT300—Set of 2: $69.95.

## NACHO CHEESE DUSTER

The scene is a familiar one. Your host is reduced to tears because she served nacho cheese tortilla chips at her party. Now her guests all have "orange finger," her furniture is stained, and the party's ruined. Now, common car-vac technology makes this dreadful embarrassment a thing of the past. Simply pour the chips from bag DIRECTLY into the Nacho Cheese Duster and—voilà!—dust-free chips spill out the other end! Works just as well with B-B-Q chips and cheese curls. Happy snacking! HT3400—$95.95.

## MR. PÂTÉ HEAD

We've got a **HUGE** stock of these imaginative play kits stowed away and are eager to give you a chance to **ENJOY** setting up for your next party! Guaranteed to take you back to your childhood. Comes complete with funny nose, mouth, eyes, hat, and ears. Simply stick them into the goose liver at your next bash and **HEY! WHAT A RIOT! HT100**—The whole sha-bang costs only **$32.95.**

# Our Gifts are Great For Giving and Getting

## BRICK TELEVISION

Everybody knows that exposed brick is in, right? Now you can be the innest with Hamper & Trivet's own 19-inch color television mounted in an exposed brick cabinet. It's beautiful. It's durable. It's heavy. Use indoors or out. Climb under it in case of tornado; it has the civil defense seal of approval. HT11400—$5,000.95.

## UNIVERSAL GIFT!

Give the gift that weighs more than our Earth: another planet! Recipient of your choice receives official-looking certificate. Mars becomes "Property of Daniel," etc. Hurry! When we run out of planets, our offer ends. HT4000—$54,000.95.

## TAPE TAILOR

Admit it! You've got a revolving rack full of 8-track tapes from the '70s that you can't use anymore because you sold your 8-track deck at a garage sale back in '79, right? Don't despair! Once again you'll enjoy the sounds of Bread and Three Dog Night as if it were yesterday—through the miracle technology we call the Tape Tailor. Based on the principle used to narrow ties that are too wide, this handy device pares down those useless 8-tracks into sleek high-tech cassettes for use in today's compact equipment.

"And what happens when I've converted all my tapes?" you might be asking. Don't worry. The Tape Tailor has a million and one household uses. It's great for cutting cassette-shaped cookies or pressing ground beef into "cassette burgers." Makes an interesting paper cutter, too. HT4600—$329.95.

## STOWAWAY LUGGAGE

World travel is fun, exciting, and educational, but there's one major flaw: it's expensive. Well, how would you like to travel the globe to your heart's desire without worrying about the cost? It's a cinch with Stowaway Luggage! You'll be traveling first class every time. On the outside, it's a sturdy steamer trunk covered handsome, durable Naugahyde. But inside, it's a roomy traveling compartment! Complete with a comfortable seat (better than most airlines), a small reading lamp, magazine rack, snap-out toiletry packet, and even a periscope so you always know where you are. And best of all, the entire case is lead-lined so X-rays can't spoil your trip. Adjustable thermostat keeps the temperature comfy inside, even if the luggage compartment is 20 below! Easy-pull swivel casters make getting you through any terminal a breeze. HT19200— $5,899.95.

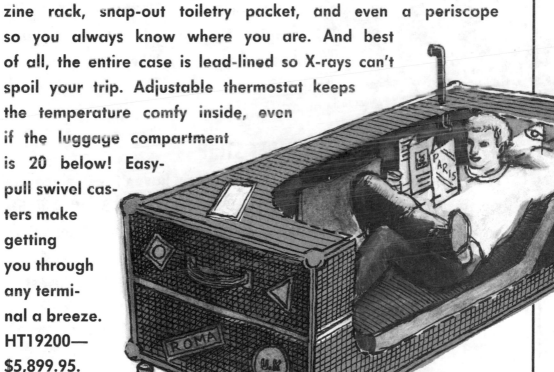

# Pet Peeves

Living with animals is at best a nuisance. Why people let pets share their lovely homes we'll never know, but there are more than a few of you out there who do, and we'd like you to buy a few things from our catalog as well.

## EXPENSIVE DOG KIT

We can't all own an Akita or a Lhasa Apso, but now we can make our little mutt look just as exotic with this do-it-yourself Expensive Dog Kit. Comes complete with swatches of wiry, tangled hair in different lengths and colors, clippers, and Everlast Epoxy. So long, Rover; hello, Tweedles. HT900—$37.95.

## NO-PET STRIP

Now you can finally visit that old friend you haven't seen since she got a dog five years ago with your H & T No-Pet Strip! A lightweight, durable ring of Plexiglas suspended from a belt keeps Fido at bay from the moment you enter your friend's home. Keeps slacks drool-proof and hair-free. Zoo keepers might do well to invest in one! HT2700—$193.95.

## PET DISH

Everybody's cuddling up to inanimate objects! But this is no rock or brick. This is a fully functional bowl, covered with a silky coat of synthetic fur. Pet it, befriend it, eat out of it! Who says you can't teach an old dog dish new tricks? HT700—$99.95.

## INFLATABLE LIVESTOCK

We've all dreamed of owning our own ranch, but the trouble of feeding and smelling large numbers of living beasts put us off. That's what led H & T to develop these realistic-looking polyurethane livestock replicas that give you all the excitement of real ranching without the messy fuss. Real wooden corral included. Available in cow, pig, and chicken. Each piece measures 18" in height. HT1800—Set of one (please specify): $59.95. Complete ranch: $2,200.95.

## HOME PET DISPLAY SYSTEM

Now you can enjoy owning pets without the hassles! With Hamper & Trivet's Patented Home Pet Display System you'll never touch the mangy critters again. Feeding tubes enter

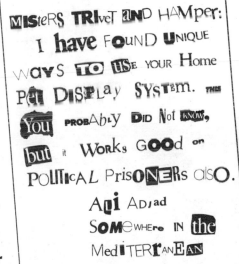

the top and waste is shuttled away in trays below. This space-age system makes it easy to keep tabs on your living property. The rotating base makes a perfect display for visitors. Great gift for people allergic to pets, afraid of pets, or who hate pets.  HT14000—$897.95.

MISteRS TRIveT aND HAMper: I have FOuND Unique wayS TO USe your Home PeT DISPLay SysTem. THIS You PROBABLY DID NOT KNOW, but it WORKS GOOd on POLITICAL PrisONErs also. Api ADIad SOMeWHEre IN the MediTERraNEan

# Sporting Goods and Sporting Betters

Sporting goods are good, but our sporting goods are better because they're great!

## FOOSBALL-ACTION PASTA SEPARATOR

You spent four years of college perfecting your foosball technique, but what have you done with it since you graduated? Nothing, right? Well, here's a chance to use that valuable "wrist action" in the kitchen. Colorful "players" kick and strain pasta noodles while you try for the winning goal. Leave it to Hamper & Trivet to fuse the delight of cooking pasta with the pulse-pounding action of foosball. Fits most huge kitchens, if you don't need a table. HT14500—$563.95.

Dear Phil and Jake,

Six months ago I was a desperate man. I had no home, no job, no girlfriend...no nothing In fact, I was in the kitchen standing on a chair with a noose around my neck when your catalog arrived and changed my life! You see, I used to be somebody. I used to have direction. But since college my life has gone downhill. You see, in college, I was a foosball champion. But as you know, after college foosball, there's no turning pro. So I drifted from odd job to odd job but nothing was the same. I kept trying to recapture past glories and failed miserably. Until I ordered the foosball action pasta seperator. Now is my life different! I own a little pasta shop in one of Boston's more fashionable districts and customers flock not only to buy pasta, but to watch me seperate it! Thanks for my life!

Bob Waystopmenjo
Boston, Mass.

## EZ-BOY SKI-LIFT MOUNT

That cold mountain wind is blowing, the line for the lift is long, the ride to the top slow and tedious, and you're wet, cold, and tired. But you feel on top of the world! You've got your EZ-Boy Ski-Lift Mount—a large, overstuffed easy chair that mounts easily onto most ski-lift benches. You'll be scaling the slope in the greatest of ease and luxury! The chair comes complete with fold-out foot rest, reclining back, and a magazine pouch. HT14600—$869.95.

## PETPAC® GOLF-MATE

This handy pet accessory will turn any decent-sized pet into a helpful golf caddy! Simply strap the Petpac® onto the back of your "best friend" and you're not only taking the ol' boy for a walk (giving him healthy exercise!); you've also got an obedient caddy that you won't have to tip! HT2500—$346.95.

## GOLF BALL FLARES

Okay, you duffers. You're out on the course, and you slice one into unpenetrable brush. How do you locate your ball? Make sure you've got a Hamper & Trivet Golf Ball Flare. Just flip a remote control toggle switch and—FOOM!—a bright red signal flare fires from the ball, rocketing hundreds of yards into the air directly overhead, making lost balls a thing of the past. Retrieve balls from up to 50 miles. Use caution in dry season, please. HT9800—One ball (all you'll ever need): $537.95.

## DECOY RACQUETS

Even if you don't play a racquet sport, the least you can do is look like it. Here's an inexpensive alternative to buying actual sports equipment—true-to-life replicas of actual racquets without the "business end." As costly as name brand gear, these handy handles protrude obviously from anything! Your pockets, gym bag, briefcase, ANYWHERE! Guaranteed to make you appear club-bound, 24 hours a day. Available in squash, tennis, and jai alai. See ya' on the courts. HT1300—$52.95.

## EXERCISE CAR

Everybody and his brother owns an exercise bike, but you can top them all with the first ever Exercise Car. Outside it's an expensive BMW; inside, we've replaced the cushy interior and powerful engine with pedals and a chain hooked up to a tension bar. Get more exercise than with a standard bike; this is a car. Use in conjunction with H & T's Motion Screen and really feel like you're getting a workout. HT20000—$56,000.95.

## THE HAMPER & TRIVET CEDAR LOG BIKE KIT

Anyone can own a log home, but how about a real 10-speed . . . made of wood! You get a complete kit—unfinished, hand-split cedar logs and all necessary hardware. Did Lincoln tour America this way? We can only wonder . . . HT4600— $459.95.

# So What's Cooking?

All us human beings share one thing in common: if we don't eat, we die. So let Hamper and Trivet turn your quest for survival into a happy-go-lucky romp, with these . . .

## COVERED SATELLITE DISH

H & T proclamation: From now on, "bring a covered dish" will really mean "Let's pick up Australian TV!" Makes perfect casseroles and picks up 137 different channels. Made of a lightweight plastic so advanced we can't even spell it. Comes in classic Corning blue on white pattern. HT8300—$195.95.

## SPRAY-CAN KITCHEN

Cooking enters the space age! Imagine virtually every conceivable condiment found in today's kitchen available in an aerosol spray can! Everything from ketchup to mustard to grape jam to hot sauce. Just shake, hold upright 6 inches from surface, and press the button. No dripping, no knives to clean. Just deliciously augmented food. HT3700—$246.95. 36 cans complete.

## THE OMELET BINDER

Why spend hundreds of dollars on a gourmet omelet class and never have anything to show for it? Now there's a way to save those precious few "perfect" omelets: the Omelet Binder. Preserve memories, settle bets! Covered in 100% virgin Sleekra® so kitchen stains wipe right off. Adjusts to accommodate crepes. HT900—$167.95.

## CROISSANWRENCH

"Wrench" those few stubborn croissants off the cookie sheet with this superbly crafted kitchen utensil. The insulated grip is a close-to-perfect replica of flaky, light pastry. But don't bite it! It's ceramic. HT300—Set of two: $79.00.

## BIG-SCREEN OVEN

Dinner and TV go together. Now, instead of watching TV at dinner, watch dinner at dinner! Your beautifully prepared meals no longer take a back seat to Wink Martindale or "Hogan's Heroes" reruns! Your supper's the star! Large 6' x 8' magnification screen attaches easily to any household oven or microwave. Makes any meal—in the immortal words of Ed Sullivan—a "really big shoe!" You'll look forward to baking again. HT2300—$358.95.

## THE CEREAL SAVER

How many times has this happened to you? You have just poured milk on your cereal when the phone rings (that important call!); you rush off to answer, only to return to an unappetizing bowl of soggy flakes or puffs. Get the Cereal Saver and never again suffer the sorrow of soggy cereal. Depressing the chrome-plated lever raises your cereal safely above the milk on a sheet of stainless steel mesh. Dishwasher safe! HT1300—$87.95 per bowl.

## SCRATCH-'N'-SNIFF PLACEMATS

Turn off the appetites of unexpected guests who've invited themselves in at mealtime. Just use these Scratch-'N'-Sniff placemats. Guests scratch the appealing strawberry and—rabbit cage! Or, how about those yummy-looking grapes? Oh, no! Wet pooch! Whoops. Try the rose—diaper bin! The Tall Ships? Ach! Summer dumpster! Recent scientific development makes it all possible, use after use after use. Guaranteed to turn moochers' stomachs. Fun to watch! HT19700—Set of eight mats: $435.95.

# *Beach Bathroom Bingo!*

You're all washed up—inside and out! Here's an exquisite collection of items for the bath and items for the beach. See if you can tell which are which . . .

## BEACH-THONG SILENCERS

Sure, summer demands that you wear those clumsy flip-flopping beach thongs. But do they have to be so NOISY?! No. Not if you slip on these deluxe Thong Silencers. Large foam-rubber "out shoes" muffle that annoying slap-slap-slap on the beach, pool-side, patio . . . anywhere. Keep feet toasty warm, too! HT2000—$67.95.

## THE TAN-THROUGH PAPERBACK

A revolutionary printing process helps you achieve the perfect all-over tan! Avoid that dreaded white rectangular spot left from a day at the beach with ordinary paperbacks. The Tan-Through Paperback lets the sun shine through! Caution: Sun Protection Factor depends on length of book. Sample titles: *Telescope Making for Beginners* and *The 1982 Chrysler LeBaron Owners Manual*. HT200 —$45.95 per copy.

## STOLEN HOTEL TOWEL & SOAP SET

"Hey, I didn't know you were a world traveler!" Imagine hearing *that* coming from your bathroom whenever you have guests over—even if you've never traveled out of state! It's a sure thing with H & T's extensive collection of hotel towels and soap from famous International Hotels. The Riviera. Rio. Paris. Reflect your would-be worldliness. "Soak" up the admiration. It's that easy! HT2400—One full suitcase: $650.95.

## DENTAL SANDER

Here's a strikingly effective new way to fight "plaque and tartar." Simply plug in the sculpted handle, insert sanding wheel in desired grain, and ZZZZZZ! You've got a bone-white smile guaranteed to stir envy in all! Simple, quick, virtually painless, and—best of all—no messy toothpaste needed! HT1400—$679.95.

## ELECTRIC TOWEL

Just plug in this plush terry-cloth towel and dry yourself off—instantly! These thirsty towels come in three styles: striped, paisley, and the Tall Ships. Perfect for the bathroom or the beach! UL approved. HT700—$79.95.

## DOPE-ON-A-ROPE

Those zip-lock baggies work fine for toting your "Mary Jane" to the Dead concert, drive-ins, the park at lunch time—but how about when you're showering? Now that's a problem. Or was until now! Introducing H & T's Dope-On-A-Rope—your own personal stash, dangling from a length of cute lime-green yarn. Keeps dryness in, moisture out. HT500—$65.95.

## POSTURE-RITE COMMODE

Everyone's getting good posture! Why not you? You've probably seen those funny-looking chairs that are supposed to help your back while you work. They really DO work. But what's the point if you go and ruin your posture everytime you "use the restroom?" With the Posture-Rite Commode you won't! This porcelain beauty is molded to the exact specifications of those chairs, making bad posture "in there" impossible. From the moment of installation you'll feel it starting to work its magic. HT8600—$3,435.95.

# We Smile Every Time You Buy Something!

## COIN TAPE

Embarrassed by loose change jingling in your pockets? There's a shockingly simple answer to this problem—H & T's Coin Tape. Strips of double-sided adhesive tape placed down the seam of your trousers or skirt allow change, tokens, loose keys to be stuck easily within arm's reach. And no more jingling! Not only that but it's a bold fashion statement everyone knows is cool. Didn't Elvis wear studs down *his* thigh? HT1700—$69.95 a roll.

## H & T's "MOST WANTED GIFT"

Here's a chance to make your friends and family wanted felons for a week—all for grins! Don't confuse this high-quality practical joke with other cheap novelty printing gimmicks! Through this special arrangement law enforcement officials actually "want" your relatives. Follow the story on the news. For more fun offer to hide your "fugitive-from-justice" in the basement; after a week, let them in on the gag! It's a blast. HT1000—$2,543.95 plus bail.

## THE ULTIMATE LOCK

This lock is unpickable, uncutable, unbreakable—even the key that comes with it won't open it. The best lock you can buy. Keeps things securely locked—forever. HT700—$187.95.

## TRENDI-SCAPE HEDGE BOWLS

Trimming hedges—what a bore; you snip, snip, snip trying to get a nice even cut, only to end up with a mere fraction of the bush you started with. And it's tedium fit for a slave! Now with H & T's chic Trendi-Scape Hedge Bowls, anyone can be a master grounds-keeper with little or no effort. Place one of the trendy new designs on your shrub and *zip!* You're cutting like a professional landscaper. Those high-quality bowls could also make you some extra $$$. HT18800—$456.95.

## TRENDI-COIF HAIR BOWLS

You've heard the old joke about cutting hair by placing a bowl on the person's head, right? Well, it's not a joke anymore! Not with H & T's incredibly chic Trendi-Coif Hair Bowls. Makes everyone a master hair stylist! Place one of the trendy new designs on the person's head and *zip!* You're cutting like a professional stylist. These high-quality bowls could make you some extra $$$. HT1000 —Set of 15 "styles": $342.95.

# That Space Behind Your House

Where do American families go in the summer? The backyard, of course. But we don't call it that. We like to be as unique and unpredictable as any of our high-quality gifts, so we'll call it "that space behind your house" and you'll know what we're talking about.

## LAWN DYE

Used to be your lawn was just like *everyone's*. Green. No room for originality there, right? Wrong! Not since we developed this revolutionary Lawn Dye. Simply screw the canister on to the end of your hose and water the lawn. Overnight you'll have a lawn that stands out in a crowd! Choose from lemon yellow, vibrant orange, hot pink, or to keep them guessing, a bright lime green. ("Something's different about the Johnson's lawn, but I just can't place it.") Make your yard the topic of discussion around the entire neighborhood! One application lasts years. Don't delay, dye today! HT1400— $398.95.

## MOIST BLANK-ETTE

Barbecues! Man, are they messy! And those moist towelettes, sheesh!—who ever thought those dinky little things could handle a goopy mess like fried chicken?! Well, picnics can be clean as a whistle from now on with H & T's Moist Blank-ettes. Each individually wrapped Blank-ette is moist and fragrant just like those smaller towelettes . . . but these are HUGE! The 6' x 6' surface cleans 6 pair of sticky hands at once, or the whole body of one extremely zealous picnic-goer. Comes in easy-to-open foil packet. HT700—$45.95 each.

## ZAP-WARE PICNIC PLATES

The only problem with eating outside is that bugs often live up to their name. And that means landing on your food. Stop them dead in their flight path with these ingenious picnic plates armed with a special feature—that popular bug-zap technology already in use on thousands of patios and poolsides. Bugs see your food, swoop down to land, and—*zap!*—they're dead. Bon appétit! HT11700—$460.95 set of eight plates.

## GARDEN HAT

*Another fine gift for your head.*

Consider the functional perfection of the fishing hat. Every tool you need is right there just above your brow. Now picture using that same simple principle in a gardening hat. A rake, a hoe, and a shovel all rest within easy reach. If you can scratch your head, getting a hand on these tools is no problem. If you've wanted a fishing cap, but hate fishing (and love gardening), then we've made your day. Extra feature! A 12-gallon leaf bag is built right into the top. HT20100—A super deal at $564.95.

## BEEF BLOCKS

Hey, *everybody* knows how much steak costs these days. Why not use the conspicuous priciness of meat to show off your wealth . . . by building with it! Use these cryogenically frozen blocks of meat to pave your drive, erect a low wall for your garden, even build a tool shed. Your neighbors can't help but notice! Especially when summer arrives. Beef up your estate *and* your image. HT800—$65.95 per lb.

# You Don't Need a Passport to Enter Our World of Gifts!

## STAINED GLASSES

Everyone knows the incredible power of stained glass to conjure up feelings of heavenliness. Well, here's a chance to have that serene feeling *all day long*. High-quality frames sport finely hand-crafted stained-glass windows, detailed down to the Last Supper. Uplifting mosaics of roses, religious icons, and the Tall Ships color your world. Enjoy this simple way to "see the Light." HT12000—$239.95 per pair.

## IMPORTED DENTAL TORTES

Give the great-tasting treat . . . that won't rot their teeth! Alternate layers of delicate chocolate mousse cake and fluffy cream laced with gritty fluoride provide the ultimate in tooth-decay prevention. You'll feel guilty and want to rush into the bathroom and brush your teeth immediately after eating one, but, without thinking, you'll be "brushing your teeth" with every delicious bite! Perfect for that person on your gift list who has a sweet tooth and wants to keep it. Available in a decorative tin with "olde tyme" dental equipment enameled in 4 brilliant colors on the sides. HT700—$265.95. (Add $342.95 for decorative tin.)

*Another fine gift for your head.*

## THE AD-VISOR

Everyone's getting into the advertising game. Cabs, buses, airplanes . . . and you! Through this unique offer, you, too, can sell out to capitalism in a big way. We'll set you up in business for yourself —with our Ad-Visor. Works like any ordinary visor, except that advertising messages crawl across a lightweight screen mounted on the front. Always tasteful, the advertising crawls across your forehead at an easily readable pace in brilliant red LED display. As easy as wearing a hat! Just put it on and watch the attention you get! Comes in four sporty colors. HT1400—$765.95.

*Another fine gift for your head.*

## SCALP VAULT

The wave of the future in personal-valuables security! Here's a safe that looks like an ordinary toup. Only you know its secret. Perfect for hiding money, small documents, and other slim belongings. Any obvious lumps or bumps can be explained away with "medical reasons." HT1500—$478.95.

# We're Steer Crazy!

We think Americans spend more time in their cars than in any other room in their house. So pull over and check out these fine items for your car.

## PORTABLE "TIP 'ER ON TWO" RAMP

You're searching desperately for a parking space—any parking space. There's one! But, oh-no! Some unthinking oaf took up two spaces! What a blockhead. If you could only park on two wheels ... With the Portable "Tip 'Er on Two" auto ramp you can! Easily pull into the tightest spaces. Great for parking around malls, making narrow escapes from pursuers, or just plain hotdogin' it. Fits in most trunks. HT17600—$2,560.95.

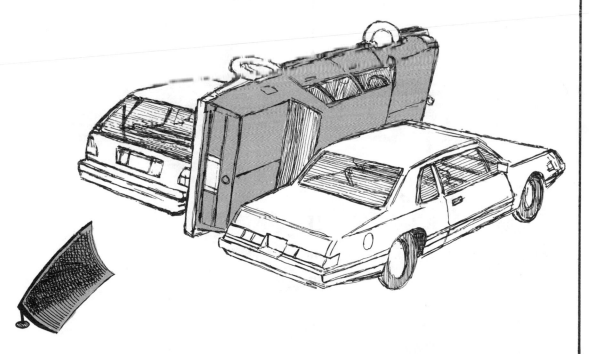

## CAR DIVIDERS

It's Sunday and time for a family drive . . . but who wants to be bothered by a bunch of screaming kids? Now you can drive in complete privacy with Car Dividers—fold-up foam insulated walls, designed to block all noise, especially high-pitched screams. Built to fit most American and foreign cars. To hell with them, you'll pull over when *you* need to go! Please specify car model and year. Available in wood paneling, stucco, and brick. HT8700—$335.95.

## CAR LOCATOR

This 6′ 2″ man straps easily to the top of any car and shouts a clear "Over here!" to signal your car's whereabouts. One arm can be left free for optional visual cue. State-of-the-art in car location technology. Hamper & Trivet not responsible for care and maintenance. HT34000—$60,650.95 each.

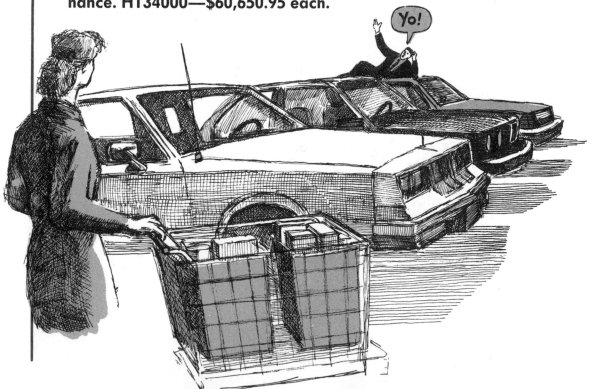

## THE MOST EXPENSIVE NO-SPILL AUTO MUG

For years engineers have worked to develop systems that help keep skyscrapers from swaying in high winds. Now, this same technology can be found in our car mug! The secret? A tuned mass damper as found in the base of New York's Citicorp building, only smaller. Simply fill your mug with coffee and rest it anywhere in your car: the dash, the door of the glove compartment, or that hump thing. Then just drive away! When you veer your car in any direction and the mug begins to sway, the hydraulic pump elevates a concrete block allowing the base to shift underneath while nitrogen-charged springs restrain the block. Servo-hydraulic actuators push block in the direction opposite to mug's movement. The result? No messy spills! Comes in three styles: "World's Best Mom," "I'm the Boss!," and "I ♥ cats." HT3000—$45,499.95 each.

## PERSONAL TRAFFIC REPORT

There's one major flaw with radio traffic reports, they don't always pertain to *you*. Heck, their whirlybird may be on the other side of town when you most need to know what the traffic situation is right in front of you. Now you can always be abreast of the situation with the Personal Traffic Report. This pint-sized traffic chopper easily attaches to the roof of any car with a 20' nylon tether. You'll receive constantly updated "synth-voice" reports at the push of a button. You'll be kept informed of such important facts as "looks clear," "congested ahead," or "I'm tangled in the phone wires." Comes complete. HT2100—$979.95.

## MOTION SCREEN

You've seen those old movies where people appear to be driving in cars, but *you* know they're actually sitting in front of a projection screen. Imagine having the same technology to work for you the next time you're in a traffic jam! We did more than imagine this: we *did* it. From four specially designed screens, your car appears to be moving in a variety of driving situations. Choose from Country Road, City-scape, Gangster Chase, and Freeway Smash-Up. It's fun *and* exciting. Perfect for livening up those long, dull road trips. Get one for every car in the family. HT40000—$9,000.95.

## CAR MOWER KIT

Tired of pushing that mower over acres and acres of lawn, but think those little mini-tractors look dumb? Wouldn't you rather mow your lawn in the air-conditioned comfort of your own car? If the answer to these questions is YES then consider Hamper & Trivet's Do-It-Yourself Car Mower Kit. Converts any regular car into a "riding" mower in just hours with tools found around any machine shop. What's more, you can still use your car for regular street driving, provided there is NO DEBRIS OF ANY KIND IN THE ROAD! Sorry, no foreign cars may be adapted. HT15700—$4,567.95.

## "STAY AWAKE" DRIVING BRACE

You've seen those little beepers that buzz when your head tilts to keep you awake while you're driving; they're not exactly fail-safe. If you're a heavy sleeper, some namby-pamby beep won't arouse you. And you don't want to be awakened by the crash of the guard rail and smash of a tree ripping your car in two like a crude can opener, do you? You should own a device that *guarantees* you won't fall asleep at the wheel—namely our "Stay Awake" Driving Brace. This amazing device holds that pesky Sandman at bay for as long as you're at the wheel. Brace attaches easily to your shoulders and holds a .357 Magnum inches from your delicate earworks. If your head so much as tilts 2.2 mm either way—BANG!—the gun off (don't worry, it's just a blank) and its piercing blast—loud enough to wake the dead—rips through the fabric of your very existence. No more sleepy head. HT6700—$1,995.95.

# Tech the Halls!

Forget the holly! That's for the birds. You're living in the '80s and that means you need as much high-tech equipment as you can squeeze between those four walls you call your fine home.

## "COMPUTER AGE" CONVERSION RACK

Look smart! This handsome oak-plated table will convert any ordinary typewriter and television into . . . a computer! Well, of course, it's not really a computer, but it looks like one; in the '80s, that's all that really counts, right? Right! No one will be the wiser, and you'll be able to easily watch your favorite shows as you type-type-type away! HT3200—$879.95.

## PULLOVEROID CAMERA

It's a sweater. A nice one, too. But what's more, it's got a fully functional instant camera sewn right in to the front. You'll love how easy it is to take pictures with one of these babies. Who wants to lug swinging bulky equipment on long straps? Thanks to this garment, no one will ever mistake you for Joe-Tourist! Just pull the wool over your eyes and snap away! S, M, L, X-L. HT2400—$457.95.

## CREPE-MATE FRY PAN

Hamper & Trivet brings human voice synthesis into the kitchen! Your car talks, your camera talks . . . why not get advice on something that's *really* hard to do: cook crepes. Our friendly fry pan talks you through the perfect crepes every time. "Don't flip 'em yet." "Lovely texture; you're a real pro." "Check the ceiling, guy." And, yes, it's no-stick. HT1600—$103.95.

## "FRUITMAN"
## PERSONAL FRUIT EAVESDROP DEVICE

This ingenious, high-tech probe picks up the myriad
sounds present in common citrus fruit. Lightweight
headphones deliver high-quality stereophonic
sounds of larva munching, juices coursing,
etc. Let "nature's music" soothe you,
excite you, gross you out. HT5200—
$325.95.

## "FALSE ALARM" CLOCK

Here's a great gift for that heavy sleeper in your home. Unlike most
alarm clocks, this one doesn't ring—in the home, that is. This alarm
rings down at police headquarters, bringing two carloads of angry
cops pounding on your door. If this doesn't wake your slumbering
wife or hubby . . . they're dead. Can also be wired into local fire
department or emergency squad alarm systems for equal effective-
ness. HT2800—$450.00.

## FIREPLACE MIKES

Can't make a decent fire? We can't help you there, but we can
make the puny fire you do manage to strike up *sound* like a roaring
blaze. These highly sensitive omni-directional heat-resistant mikes
are great for amplifying the sounds of a fireplace. Just turn up the
volume and WOW! Makes even the most embarrassingly small twig
glow sound like the very fires of HELL! Guaranteed to raise your
temperature just from hearing it. HT4200—$1,457.95.

## HOME LAUGH-TRACK

Yes! Your life can be as fulfilling as those you watch unfurl on TV. Now every family can be funny and entertaining. Simply flip a switch and even the weakest, most idiotic joke told by any member of your family becomes a laugh riot! Also available in Soap Opera (Harp Glissandos) and TV Movie of the Week (Melodramatic). HT1600—Entire system installed $562.95.

Dear Phil & Jake

I used to think my parents were drones. Real morons, you know? I didn't want to be seen with them in public, let alone have to put up with them in private, but since I'm only eight I don't have much choice. But let me tell you, your HOME LAUGH TRACK changed my young life! Now, I can't wait to get home! It's like being in a weekly sit-com ... every night. Dad is always a riot and those one liners of Mom's just kill me! We're thinking of pitching our "show" to ABC.
What do you think?

Debbie Dejeerling
Studio City,
Calif.

# More Letters From Our Satisfied Customers Like You Could Be

USA 22¢

Phil and Jake

Sirs:
I was very pleased with the products I ordered from your catalog. I really think you guys are great. In fact, I, I ... I Love You. I'd do anything for you. I'm sending away every issue of your catalog ... I mean it. I'm getting my new babies ... the old one. I'm conducting readings every Wednesday. I'm getting up a petition to damn the dance of my state. I live only for the day I meet you.
Your Servant forever,
Rory Huckleburger
Webb's Bowl,
Chicago, Hamper & Trivet Cal.

Dear Sirs,
I was given the gift of the Stolen Hotel Towel and Soap Set and now I feel like a real world traveller! I think its great. It opened a whole new world for me. Now I pretend all day about getting out of the house and going to all those exotic places. They're really given me something to live for. Sometimes I even take along my imaginary friends with me. Thanks again. And my parents want me to thank you for the Ultimate Lock.
Yours,
Jimmy
I'm not sure where but its cool

Phil Hamper +
Jake Trivet
U.S.A.

Dear Hamper & Trivet:
We just opened our shipment from your ▮▮▮ company and found everything is ▮▮ what we ordered. I have half a mind to think you guys ought to be ▮▮ the authorities. I won't rest until I see you ▮▮.
Mr & Mrs. Milton
Akron, Ohio

Dear Sirs:
I don't usually shop by catalog. They're run by cheap swindlers and rip off artists. Their gifts are not high quality. But I have to hand it to you boys, you're tops in my catalog! Your stuff is great and when I say something, I mean it! Just two suggestions though, personally, I'd like to see more Santa heads (even in summer) and how about a page of 88¢ items? It gets them every time!
Sincerely,
John Spencer
John Spencer
President, Spencer Gifts

# *About the Authors*

After a strikingly normal childhood and a four-year stint at Ohio University, where he received a degree in advertising, Mark Drop moved to New York City to make it big as a copywriter. Since his arrival in 1983, he's pretty much forgotten all that nonsense and busied himself with writing plays, rock songs, and this book.

Steven Spiegel graduated from Ohio University with a degree in theatre and moved to New York City where he found no work. Being resourceful, he entered the world of advertising, which is kind of like the theatre except there's no curtain. Since then he has written an award-winning ad for the Statue of Liberty and two children's television specials for Multimedia Entertainment. He also continues to write plays and makes no money at it.